Pebble® Plus

Dinosaurs and Prehistoric Animals
Megalosaurus

by Janet Riehecky

Consulting Editor: Gail Saunders-Smith, PhD

Consultant: Jack Horner, Curator of Paleontology
Museum of the Rockies
Bozeman, Montana

Capstone press®

Mankato, Minnesota

Pebble Plus is published by Capstone Press,
151 Good Counsel Drive, P.O. Box 669, Mankato, Minnesota 56002.
www.capstonepress.com

1 2 3 4 5 6 14 13 12 11 10 09

Library of Congress Cataloging-in-Publication Data
Riehecky, Janet, 1953–
    Megalosaurus / by Janet Riehecky.
    p. cm. — (Pebble Plus. Dinosaurs and prehistoric animals)
    Summary: "Simple text and illustrations present megalosaurus, how it
looked, and what it did" — Provided by publisher.
    Includes bibliographical references and index.
    ISBN-13: 978-1-4296-0039-2 (hardcover)
    ISBN-10: 1-4296-0039-X (hardcover)
    1. Megalosaurus — Juvenile literature. I. Title.
QE862.S3R536 2009
567.912 — dc22   2006102215

Editorial Credits
Sarah L. Schuette and Jenny Marks, editors; Gene Bentdahl, designer;
    Wanda Winch, photo researcher

Illustration and Photo Credits
Jon Hughes, illustrator
Wikipedia/Ballista, Oxford University Museum of Natural History, London, 21

Note to Parents and Teachers

The Dinosaurs and Prehistoric Animals set supports national science standards related
to the evolution of life. This book describes and illustrates the megalosaurus. The
images support early readers in understanding the text. The repetition of words and phrases
helps early readers learn new words. This book also introduces early readers to subject-specific
vocabulary words, which are defined in the Glossary section. Early readers may need assistance
to read some words and to use the Table of Contents, Glossary, Read More, Internet Sites, and
Index sections of the book.

Table of Contents

megalosaurus (MEG-ah-low-SORE-us)

Great Lizard

Megalosaurus was the first dinosaur to be given a name. Megalosaurus means "great lizard."

Megalosaurus lived

in prehistoric times

about 170 million years ago.

It roamed Europe.

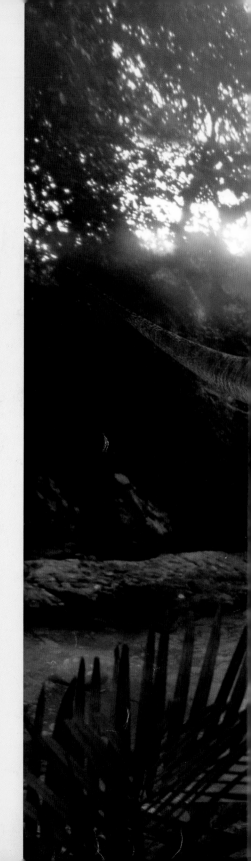

How Megalosaurus Looked

Megalosaurus was

about the size of a small bus.

It stood 10 feet (3 meters) tall.

It was 30 feet (9 meters) long.

Megalosaurus had two legs.

It walked with its toes

pointed in.

Megalosaurus had
a huge tail.
Its tail stuck straight out
when it walked.

Megalosaurus had hands

with three fingers.

Each finger had

a hooked claw.

What Megalosaurus Did

Megalosaurus may have
hunted in packs.

It chased large plant eaters.

Megalosaurus may have

jumped on its prey.

It took big bites

with its sharp teeth.

The End of Megalosaurus

Megalosaurus died out

about 155 million years ago.

No one knows why.

You can see its fossils

in museums.

Glossary

claw — a hard, curved nail on the foot of an animal

fossil — the remains or traces of an animal or a plant, preserved as rock

hunt — to chase and kill animals for food

museum — a place where objects of art, history, or science are shown

pack — a group of animals that hunts together

prehistoric — very old; prehistoric means belonging to a time before history was written down.

prey — an animal that is hunted for food

Read More

Dixon, Dougal. *The Illustrated Encyclopedia of Dinosaurs.* London: Anness Publishing, Ltd., 2006.

Gray, Susan H. *Megalosaurus.* Chanhassen, Minn.: Child's World, 2005.

Richardson, Hazel. *Dinosaurs and Prehistoric Life.* Smithsonian Handbooks. N.Y.: Dorling Kindersley, 2003.

Internet Sites

FactHound offers a safe, fun way to find educator-approved Internet sites related to this book.

Here's what to do:

1. Visit *www.facthound.com*

2. Choose your grade level.

3. Begin your seach.

This book's ID is 9781429600392.

FactHound will fetch the best sites for you!

Index

Word Count: 131
Grade: 1
Early-Intervention Level: 16